SHARKS

HAMMERHEAD SHARK

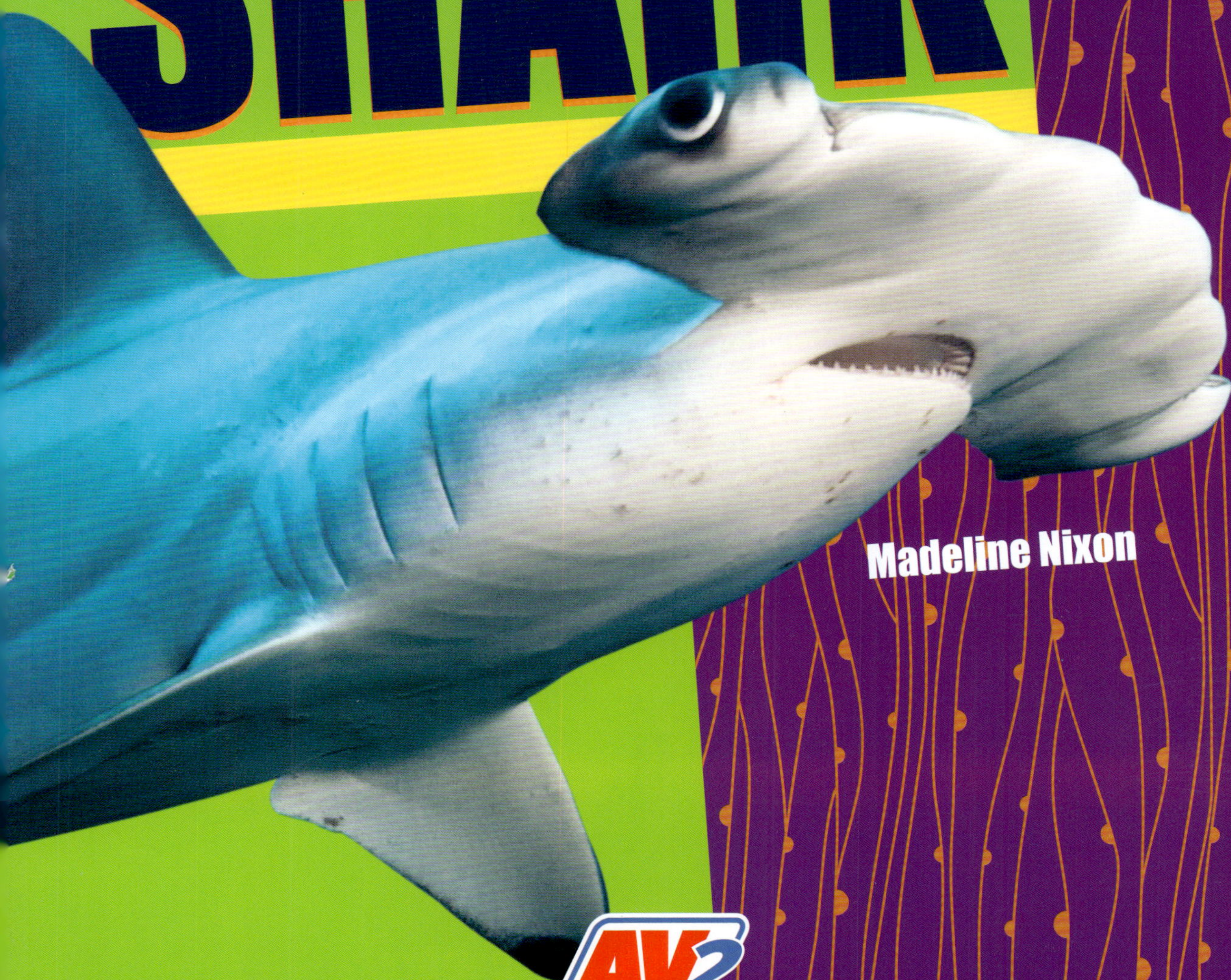

Madeline Nixon

AV2

www.av2books.com

Step 1
Go to **www.av2books.com**

Step 2
Enter this unique code
COHELWG6C

Step 3
Explore your interactive eBook!

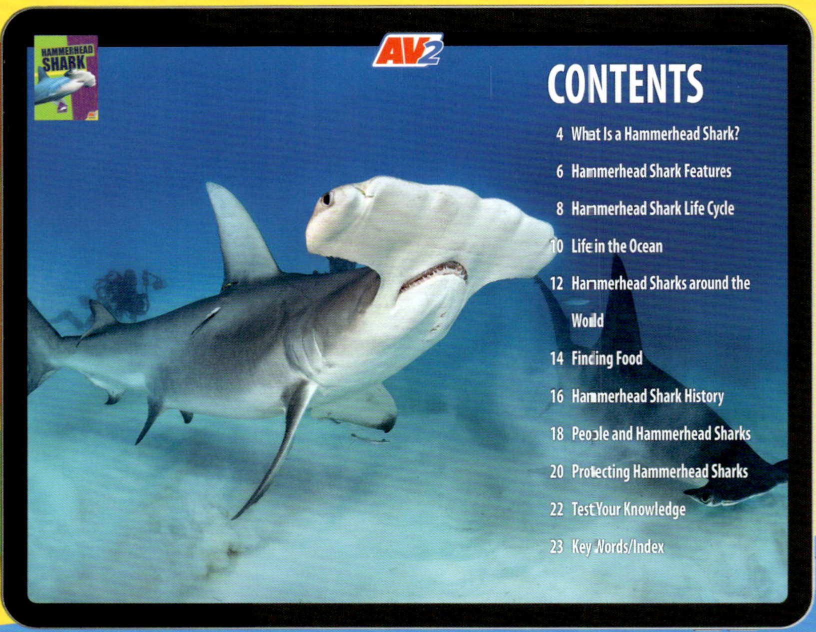

AV2 is optimized for use on any device

Your interactive eBook comes with...

Contents
Browse a live contents page to easily navigate through resources

Audio
Listen to sections of the book read aloud

Videos
Watch informative video clips

Weblinks
Gain additional information for research

Try This!
Complete activities and hands-on experiments

Key Words
Study vocabulary, and complete a matching word activity

Quizzes
Test your knowledge

Slideshows
View images and captions

... and much, much more!

SHARKS

HAMMERHEAD SHARK

CONTENTS

What Is a Hammerhead Shark?

A hammerhead shark gets its name from the shape of its head. It looks like a hammer, with eyes on either end. There are nine types of hammerhead sharks. Some have heads that look like bonnets. Others have heads that are **scalloped**.

Three types of hammerheads are **endangered**. They are the scalloped, winghead, and great hammerheads. The great hammerhead shark is the largest of the hammerhead sharks.

"Hammerheads are special fish, and there is nothing that remotely resembles them anywhere on the planet."

—Andrew Martin, Evolutionary Biologist at University of Colorado at Boulder

Great Hammerhead Shark

Scientific Name
Sphyrnidae mokarran

Diet Carnivore

Size 13–20 feet (4–6.1 meters)

Weight 500–1,000 pounds (227–454 kilograms)

Conservation Status Critically Endangered

Population Unknown

Hammerhead Shark Features

Hammerhead sharks have several features that help them live. Some help them to see better and stay safe. Others help them to hunt.

Skin

The skin of a hammerhead shark is covered with millions of scales called **denticles**. They look like teeth. Denticles protect the shark's skin.

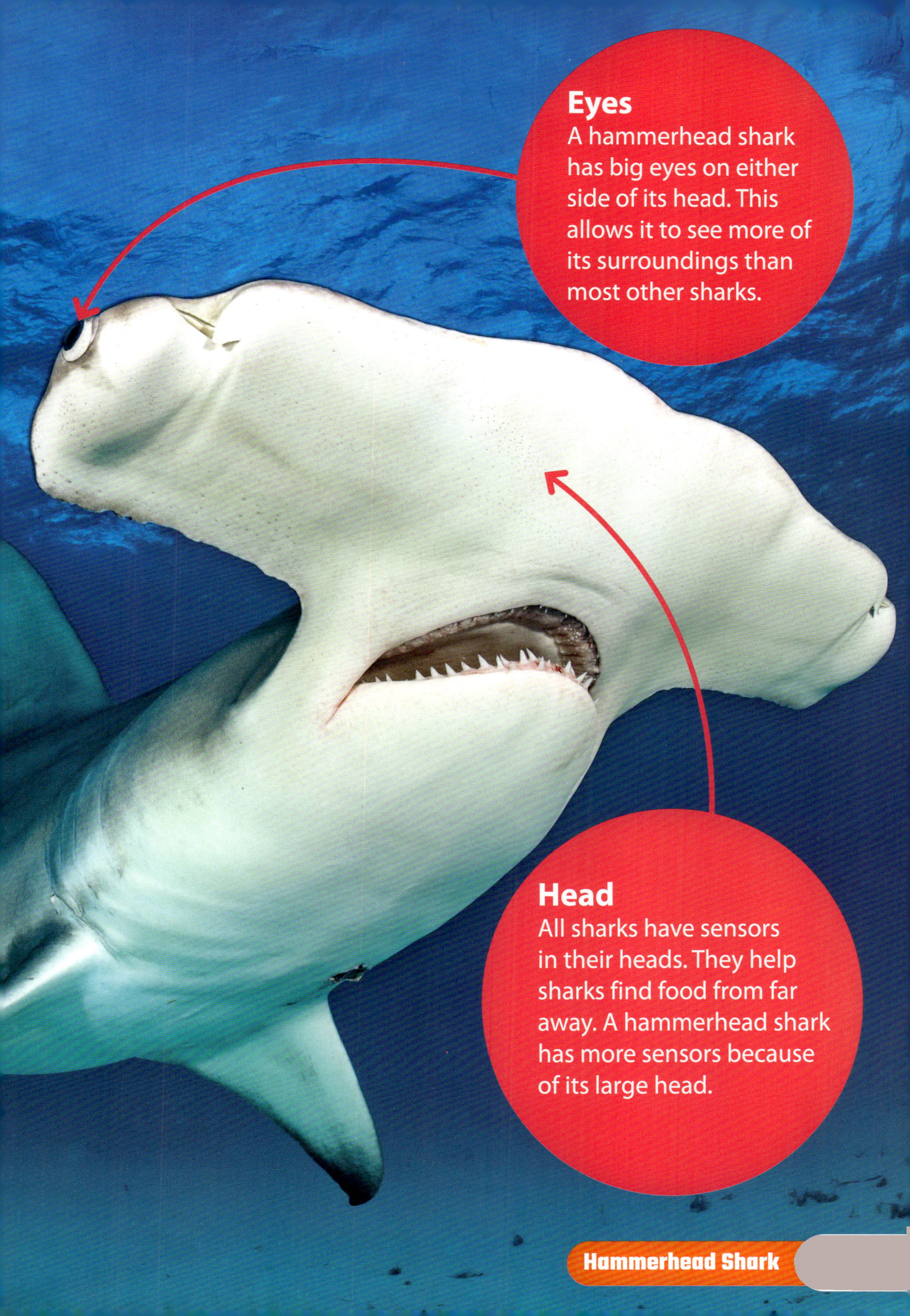

Eyes
A hammerhead shark has big eyes on either side of its head. This allows it to see more of its surroundings than most other sharks.

Head
All sharks have sensors in their heads. They help sharks find food from far away. A hammerhead shark has more sensors because of its large head.

Hammerhead Shark Life Cycle

A female hammerhead shark can be pregnant every two years. She gives birth to live shark pups. There can be 6 to 42 pups in one **litter**. Baby hammerhead sharks need to watch out for adults. They may eat younger sharks. Hammerhead sharks can live more than 20 years.

How Big Are Sharks?

Life in the Ocean

Hammerhead sharks like warm water. However, they **migrate** to cooler waters during the summer. Most often, they live near coastlines. Sometimes, they are found far offshore. Hammerhead sharks spend their time on the water's **surface** or on the ocean floor.

SHARK BITES

Great hammerhead sharks **migrate** up to **756 miles (1,200 km)** during the **summer**.

Hammerhead Sharks around the World

Different kinds of hammerhead sharks live in different parts of the world. However, most stay in warm, shallow waters.

1 Bimini, Bahamas

There are many great hammerhead sharks off the coast of Bimini. Through December to April, the Bimini Scuba Center offers dives to see them.

2 Red Sea, Egypt

Scalloped hammerhead sharks are commonly found in the Red Sea. There are so many that several dive centers offer dive tours just to see them.

3 Philippines

Many people in the Philippines are worried because the winghead shark is endangered. They want worldwide protection for these sharks.

Finding Food

Hammerhead sharks eat only meat. This makes them **carnivores**. Stingrays, shellfish, squid, and octopuses are their main food. Hammerheads have no interest in hunting large fish like other sharks do. The largest animals they hunt are stingrays.

Since most of their **prey** is on the bottom of the ocean, that is where they hunt. Hammerhead sharks have long and jagged teeth to help them tear their food. Their hammer-shaped head helps them pin down their prey.

SHARK BITES

Hammerhead sharks are the **only sharks** that can **move** their **heads** up and **down**.

Hammerhead Shark History

Hammerhead sharks have lived on Earth for more than 20 million years. However, they were much bigger back then. Today, they have shrunk in size. This may help them to survive. They grow faster and have babies at a younger age.

Theodore Gill discovered the hammerhead shark in 1872.

People and Hammerhead Sharks

Hammerhead sharks are not dangerous to people. Their mouths are small and face down. This makes it hard for them to attack larger animals.

There are many places around the world where shark diving is popular. Many people scuba dive to see hammerhead sharks. This is because they usually do not attack. If they feel threatened, they send off **warning signals**. Trained divers know these signs and how to stay safe.

SHARK BITES

There have been only **17 unprovoked** hammerhead **attacks** on **humans**. None have caused a **death**.

Protecting Hammerhead Sharks

Small hammerhead sharks face attacks from dolphins and orcas. Great hammerhead sharks have no predators. Humans are their only threat.

Hammerheads are hunted for their fins, oils, and **hides**. They also get caught in fishing gear meant for other fish. Several countries have banned taking hammerhead shark fins. Others have fines and prison time for people who hunt these sharks **illegally**.

The great hammerhead shark was declared critically endangered in December 2019.

Great Hammerhead Shark Conservation Status

EX	EW	CR	EN	VU	NT	LC
Extinct	Extinct in the Wild	Critically Endangered	Endangered	Vulnerable	Near Threatened	Least Concern

Test Your Knowledge

1
How long have hammerhead sharks lived on Earth?

20 million years

2
What sharks do hammerhead sharks eat?

Smaller hammerheads

3
Which types of hammerhead sharks are endangered?

Scalloped, winghead, and great

4
What is an adult great hammerhead's only threat?

Humans

5
How many types of hammerhead sharks are there?

Nine

6
Where do great hammerhead sharks migrate in the summer?

To cooler waters

7
How many pups can a female hammerhead shark give birth to?

6 to 42

8
From where do hammerhead sharks get their name?

Their hammer-shaped heads

Key Words

carnivores: animals that eat meat

denticles: tooth-shaped scales on a shark's skin

endangered: an animal at risk of disappearing from Earth

hides: skins from animals

illegally: against the law

litter: a group of animals born together

migrate: to move from one place to another

prey: an animal that is hunted by another

scalloped: an edge that has many curves

surface: the top of a body of water

warning signals: signs of alarm given by an animal

Index

Get the best of both worlds.

AV2 bridges the gap between print and digital.

The expandable resources toolbar enables quick access to content including **videos**, **audio**, **activities**, **weblinks**, **slideshows**, **quizzes**, and **key words**.

Animated videos make static images come alive.

Resource icons on each page help readers to further **explore key concepts**.

Published by AV2
350 5th Avenue, 59th Floor
New York, NY 10118
Website: www.av2books.com

Library of Congress Control Number: 2019955109

ISBN 978-1-7911-2103-7 (hardcover)
ISBN 978-1-7911-2104-4 (softcover)
ISBN 978-1-7911-2105-1 (multi-user eBook)
ISBN 978-1-7911-2106-8 (single-user eBook)

Printed in Guangzhou, China
1 2 3 4 5 6 7 8 9 0 24 23 22 21 20

022020
101119

Project Coordinator: John Willis
Designer: Terry Paulhus

Every reasonable effort has been made to trace ownership and to obtain permission to reprint copyright material. The publishers would be pleased to have any errors or omissions brought to their attention so that they may be corrected in subsequent printings.

AV2 acknowledges Getty Images, Minden Pictures, and Shutterstock as its primary image suppliers for this title.